B is for Blue Planet

An Earth Science Alphabet

Written by Ruth Strother and Illustrated by Bob Marstall

Acknowledgments

I would like to thank Donna Blevins for advising me from a teacher's perspective and
Susy Svatek Ziegler, assistant professor of Geography at the University of Minnesota, for her expertise and guidance.

— Ruth

For their invaluable support in various ways, I'm deeply grateful to Jane and Earl Soller, Don and Mary Pat Marstall,
Dave and Pat Marstall, Nancy and Frank Goad, Christopher Marstall, Jane Yolen, Larry Pringle, Patricia Lee Lewis, Jeff Dwyer,
Kristie Miner, Louise Lucht, Faith Deering, and Kasey Neiss. Special thanks to David White, Lydia Sanders Morrison,
Sky Andrews, Laurie Sanders, and Fred Morrison for their timely assistance...and others who will remain anonymous but not forgotten.

— Bob

Sleeping Bear Press™

315 East Eisenhower Parkway, Suite 200
Ann Arbor, MI 48108
www.sleepingbearpress.com

© 2011 Sleeping Bear Press is an imprint of Gale, a part of Cengage Learning.

10 9 8 7 6 5 4 3 2 1

Printed by China Translation & Printing Services Limited, Guangdong
Province, China. 1st printing. 11/2010

Library of Congress Cataloging-in-Publication Data
Strother, Ruth.
B is for blue planet : an earth science alphabet / written by Ruth Strother ; illustrated
by Robert Marstall.
p. cm.
ISBN 978-1-58536-454-1
1. Geology--Juvenile literature. 2. Earth sciences--Juvenile literature. 3. English
language--Alphabet--Juvenile literature. I. Marstall, Bob, ill. II. Title.
QE29.S795 2011
550--dc22
201003063

To my daughter, Stephanie, and my nieces
Tess, Gaby, Juliana, Clarissa, Natalie, and Louisa.

— Ruth

For Rudolph Torrini, a noted sculptor and my drawing instructor at Webster College (now Webster University).
The fires of the Renaissance burn brightly within him, and he fanned the ember he found within me.
Whatever I accomplish as an artist rests on his structural approach to observing and drawing the human figure.

— Bob

Aa

We don't really know what life was like 100 million years ago, when the dinosaurs were stomping around on Earth. But clues are sprinkled all around the world. Some clues are trapped in time capsules called amber.

Amber was formed from hardened resin produced by trees. When a branch breaks or beetles chew into bark, thick blobs of resin slowly flow out of the tree. Immediately, the resin begins to harden, forming a seal to protect the damaged wood.

Millions of years ago, flowers and leaves got stuck in the resin. Insects and spiders were also easily trapped by the sticky, gooey stuff. Instantly, the resin surrounded the unlucky critter, and death was quick. Anything trapped in resin became a perfectly preserved 3-D fossil, right down to its tiniest features.

The amber we find today is resin that dropped to the ground. Natural materials like leaves and damp soil covered the resin. It became buried in the earth, getting harder and harder. After millions of years, the resin, now called amber, was carried out to sea by rains. Eventually, it washed ashore.

Some believe that amber was the first jewelry worn by prehistoric people 30,000 years ago. We still wear amber jewelry today. But some people collect amber just to marvel over the detailed peek it gives us into the mysterious world of long ago.

A is for Amber

Yellow, red, white, and golden,
amber formed from resin olden.
Trapped in time for all to see,
look, a perfect ancient bee!

Bb

About three-quarters of the earth's surface is covered by water. From outer space, all that water makes our planet look blue. That's why Earth has been nicknamed the Blue Planet.

Most of the earth's water can be found in salty oceans. The rest is freshwater. But most freshwater is trapped in glaciers and underground. The tiny bit of freshwater left is the water we use; it is found in rivers and lakes.

A river flows from high land, down to a lake or ocean. During its journey, the river picks up and carries away pebbles, sand, and other debris called sediment. The sediment is deposited downstream when the river's flow slows. Over time, a river erodes, or wears away, the surrounding land. Rivers are one of the natural forces that change the shape of the landscape.

A lake doesn't flow like a river. Instead it is kept in place by the surrounding land. The water in a lake can seep into the ground, evaporate into the air, or flow away in a stream. To keep the lake from disappearing, it needs to get water from rain, a river, or an underground spring.

Earth is the only planet in our solar system that is covered by bodies of water. And it is the only planet that can support life—at least as far as we know!

B is for Blue Planet

Water up and water down,
        covering almost all the ground.
                Lakes and oceans, rivers, too,
        turn the earth a brilliant blue.

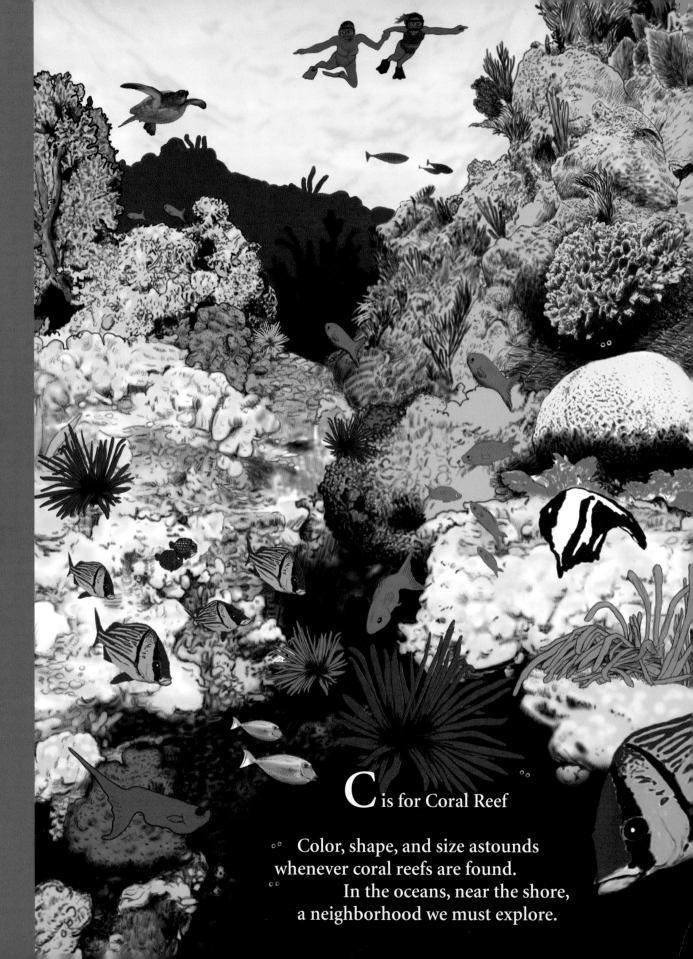

Coral reefs are the largest natural structures on Earth. So large, in fact, that they are the only living formations that can be seen from outer space. Creations this big take a long time to grow. The coral reefs we have today are 5 thousand to 50 million years old. But coral reefs are fragile. They can be destroyed quickly by a diver's touch or warming water temperatures. So what exactly is a coral reef?

Millions of tiny jellyfish-like animals called coral polyps create a coral reef. Reef-building polyps create the hard corals. Some are no bigger than the head of a pin. They attach themselves to a surface, usually a reef that already exists. Once attached, a polyp builds a cuplike structure around itself for protection. The structure is made of calcium carbonate, otherwise known as limestone. When a polyp dies, it leaves behind this limestone skeleton. Layers of limestone build over thousands of years to form the massive reefs we see today.

Coral reefs form in warm, shallow, clear ocean waters. Although they cover only a small portion of the ocean floor, coral reefs provide a rich habitat for around 25 percent of all ocean life that we know of. Scientists believe millions of unknown species of marine life have yet to be discovered living in coral reefs. Coral reefs are definitely an ecosystem worth protecting!

C is for Coral Reef

Color, shape, and size astounds
whenever coral reefs are found.
In the oceans, near the shore,
a neighborhood we must explore.

Endless sand scorched by the sun's heat: that's a desert, right? Well, yes, some deserts are like that. Dryness, though, is what really defines a desert.

In the United States, deserts are formed by the rain shadow effect. When moist air hits a barrier such as a mountain, it is forced upward. As it rises, the air cools, clouds form, and rain or snow may fall. The air is dry by the time it gets over the mountain, and a desert develops on the other side.

The desert's low humidity creates little, if any, cloud formation. One reason some deserts are so hot is that clouds aren't protecting them from the sun's rays. At night, with no blanket of humidity to trap it, the day's heat escapes into the air. The desert quickly cools. Some nights can even bring frost to a desert landscape.

At first glance a desert looks lifeless. But a great variety of plants and animals have adapted to its harsh environment. They've developed unique ways to collect and store water and to avoid or tolerate the heat. Living underground, hunting at night, growing deep or widely spread shallow roots—animals and plants have found ways to eke out a life in the stark, dry beauty of the desert.

Dd

D is for Deserts

Rain, rain, gone away,
but some plants found ways to stay.
In the desert dry and hot,
some animals also chose that spot.

E is for Earthquakes

Pushing and heaving far underground,
plates of the earth are moving around.
A sudden jolt, a roll, a shake,
no warning is given before an earthquake.

Ee

When Earth was young, its outer surface was hot, much too hot for life to exist. Eventually, the surface cooled and hardened to form the planet's crust. It didn't harden as one solid sphere, though. The surface developed cracks and separated into large slabs of rock called plates.

The plates float on molten rock. Sometimes they creep, moving slowly and steadily. But sometimes they collide, pushing and grinding against each other. When this happens, force builds until one huge slab of rock suddenly breaks or slips past another. Pent-up energy is released like the sudden uncoiling of a spring. That's what makes an earthquake.

Earthquakes don't just shake up the earth. They're a powerful force that's responsible for sculpting mountains, creating volcanoes, and triggering giant sea waves called tsunamis (soo-NAH-meez). With their land-building abilities and potential for destruction, earthquakes have inspired and befuddled scientists for years. No one has yet figured out how to predict one. With several million earthquakes estimated daily (most are too small for us to feel), there's still a lot for us to learn.

F is for Fossils

Outlining life that used to be,
fossils are a history.
A story of the earth that teemed
with plants and animals now unseen.

Ff

If there are fossils underfoot, anyone can stumble upon them when hiking down a path. You don't have to be a scientist. Fossils are the preserved remains of prehistoric plants and animals. Remains are a dead organism's body parts and traces such as footprints, dung, nests, and eggs. Many fossils represent extinct species that haven't lived on Earth for millions of years.

A plant or animal buried immediately upon death is more likely to become a fossil than one exposed to scavengers and decomposition. Remains often are buried in sand and mud. The soft parts usually rot, leaving only the hard parts such as bones, teeth, and shells. Layer upon layer of the sandy sediment pile on top of the remains over thousands of years. Eventually pressure builds and the sediment is squeezed and hardened into sedimentary rock. The remains are trapped in place.

Over time, the actual remains may be replaced by minerals, leaving a fossil that's a stone model of the real thing. Some fossils are an imprint left in the rock. And fossils can be the result of a quick freeze or a tumble into the gooey trappings of tar pits.

Long-buried fossils are brought to the surface by erosion and movements of the earth. So the next time you go hiking, keep your eyes to the ground. Who knows, you may be the next person to discover the fossil of a lost species!

Gg

Glaciers are often described as rivers of ice. And that's pretty much what they are—large bodies of ice that slowly move. But glaciers aren't ordinary ice like you see in skating rinks or in your freezer.

A glacier starts to form in areas where it's too cold for snow to completely melt. Year after year the delicate snowflakes get pressed together under the weight of new snowfall. The snow keeps falling and the older snow gets even more compressed. Air pockets between the flakes become smaller. Over time the snowflakes are transformed to rounded ice crystals. These crystals get bigger as more snow falls and compression increases. Air pockets become even smaller, and the glacier's ice takes on a blue hue.

When the ice becomes big enough and heavy enough, the pressure of its weight and the force of gravity causes it to flow. The ice is now officially a glacier.

A typical glacier flows slowly, maybe only inches a day. As it advances forward, a glacier erodes the land underneath by scraping up sand and rocks. When it retreats, or melts, it deposits the sand and rocks, leaving them behind. Glaciers have sculpted many of the valleys, lakes, ridges, and mountain peaks we see today. So it's not surprising that glaciers are considered one of nature's most powerful landscaping forces.

G is for Glaciers

Ice is flowing, groaning, creaking,
trapping boulders, rocks, and sand.
Slowly downhill it is creeping,
carving changes in the land.

A hurricane is a huge storm that forms over ocean waters. It can be hundreds of miles wide and last for more than a week. For a hurricane to develop, the water temperature has to be at least 80 degrees Fahrenheit (27 degrees Celsius). The warm, moist air that hovers and then rises over these waters is part of what energizes a hurricane.

As hurricane winds pick up, they begin to spiral inward. This motion is aided by the Coriolis force, which is caused by the rotation of the earth. Winds north of the equator, where the United States lies, spin counterclockwise toward a center of low air pressure. To be called a hurricane, winds must blow faster than 73 miles (117 kilometers) per hour.

At the center of a hurricane is the eye, which can be 5 to 120 miles (8 to 192 kilometers) across. The eye is calm, with hardly any storm activity at all. But the wall of clouds surrounding the eye is crazy with hurling rain, strong winds, and thunderstorms.

As a hurricane spins toward land, it pushes a dome of water called a storm surge onto the coast. A powerful hurricane moving inland can destroy everything in its path, but at last it can now be stopped. Once a hurricane hits land, its energy source—the ocean's warm, moist air—is gone. Soon the hurricane fizzles out.

H h

H is for Hurricanes

Storms are brewing, winds are swirling,
ocean water warms the air.
Building stronger 'til it's hurling
straight for land—oh what a scare!

Ii

Rocks come in a variety of colors, shapes, and textures. But they are all grouped into three main types—igneous, sedimentary, and metamorphic. Amazingly, any one type of rock can be changed into any other, given enough time and the right conditions. The rock cycle describes how this happens.

The heat deep inside Earth melts rock into a molten slurry called magma. Magma can stay underground. It can also make its way to the earth's surface, where it's called lava. When magma or lava cools, it becomes solid igneous rock.

As time passes, rocks wear down and erode. Bits of rock wear away and are carried off by wind and water. Eventually, they are deposited as sediment at the bottom of lakes, rivers, or oceans. Over millions of years, layers of sediment build, compact, and harden into sedimentary rock. Most of the fossils we've found have formed in sedimentary rock.

Metamorphic rock forms when other rocks are exposed to heat and pressure inside the earth. The rocks partially melt and then harden into metamorphic rock. Limestone is a sedimentary rock. When exposed to heat and pressure, limestone becomes a metamorphic rock called marble.

Movements of the earth's crust, or surface, can push rock deep enough underground for it to melt into magma again. And then the cycle continues, as it has since the time long before dinosaurs.

I is for Igneous Rock

Heated or changed or formed from debris,
three types of rock are always to be.
Here before dinosaurs, you, or me,
rocks are recycled endlessly.

J j

J is for Jurassic

A time on Earth called the Jurassic,
was nothing less than quite fantastic.
Giant sharks, sea monsters too,
joined dinosaurs—some even flew!

No one knows the exact age of the earth. How could we—it was formed about 4.5 billion years ago! There weren't even any people back then. Plants and animals didn't exist either. In fact, there was no life at all—until about 700 million years later.

Studying the history of life on Earth year by year is impossible. Instead, Earth's history is counted in millions of years by using the age of each layer of rock as a guide. The geologic time line is the result. It is divided into eons, eras, periods, epochs, and ages. Most of us know about the Jurassic period, which was about 200 million years ago. That's when dinosaurs ruled and birds first came to be.

Fast-forward about 150 million years to the ice ages of the Pleistocene epoch. Earth was mostly frozen. Dinosaurs no longer ruled— they no longer lived. Instead, giant birds and mammals like mammoths and giant sloths lumbered across the land. It wasn't until about 190,000 years ago that people came on the scene.

The last ice age ended around 10,000 years ago. Since then, Earth has become warmer and mammals have become smaller. Who knows what the earth has in store for us in the future. One thing's for certain: human life on Earth is a mere blink of an eye when measured in geologic time.

On the surface, karst looks a lot like many other landscapes. It's bumpier than most other places. And it may be more lush and beautiful than some other areas. But it's what's below the surface that really defines karst.

Beneath soil and grass and plants is bedrock. In karst, bedrock is usually limestone, but it can be any type of water-soluble rock.

Water reaches karst land by rainfall or by river. The water mixes with carbon dioxide from the air or the ground and forms carbonic acid. This acidic water seeps into the ground and trickles through cracks and spaces in the bedrock. It dissolves the rock, carving out tunnels. Slowly, over millions of years, caves, sinkholes, and springs are hollowed out. Some say karst looks like Swiss cheese covered by land. It's this dissolved bedrock that gives karst land its special bumpy appearance.

Karst isn't just stunning landscape with a maze of underground passageways. Karst caves are home to a wide variety of animal life. Artifacts from cultures of long ago can be found in the caves as well. But most important, the groundwater that flows through karst bedrock supplies about 40 percent of America's drinking water. A truly remarkable landform!

K is for Karst

Karst is land with a surprise,
streams beneath and caves inside.
Water eats away at rock,
then hollow ground is what you got.

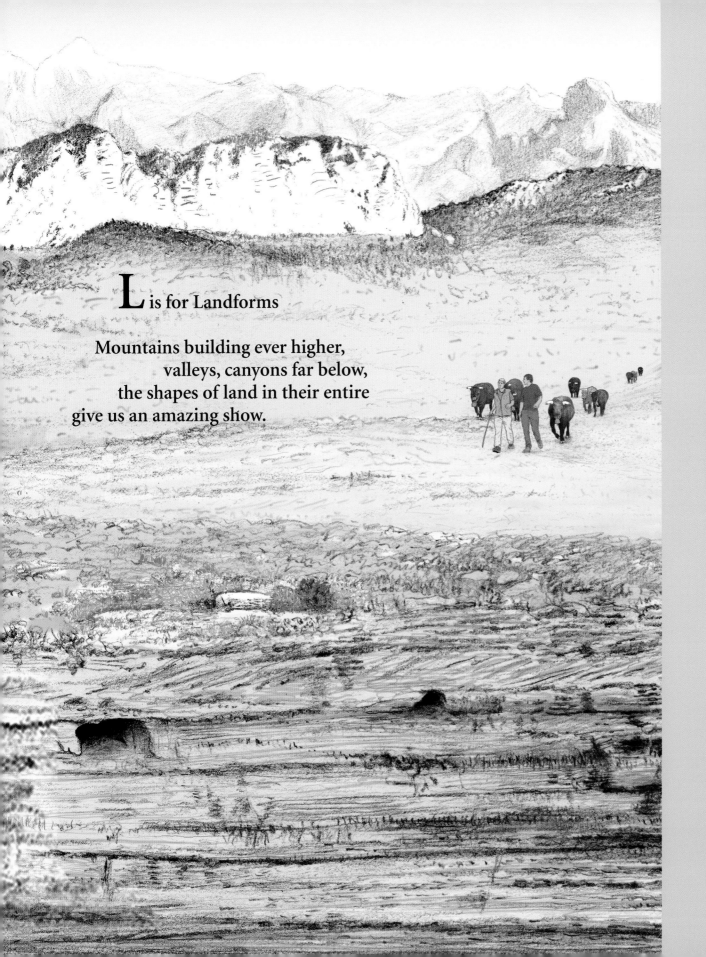

L is for Landforms

Mountains building ever higher,
valleys, canyons far below,
the shapes of land in their entire
give us an amazing show.

Land has been shaped and reshaped throughout Earth's history. It's changing right now, even as you're reading this book! Mountains, valleys, canyons, islands—all are constantly building up, wearing away, or shifting. Many forces of nature have contributed to the variety of the landforms we see today.

Most dramatic are the mountains and mountain ranges that loom above. Some mountains were formed by volcanoes. In fact, many islands were formed by the buildup of cooled and hardened lava spewed from underwater volcanoes. The islands are the tops of these volcanic mountains. Most mountains, though, were formed millions of years ago when the collision of underground plates shoved rock and land upward.

Just as the forces of nature can build, so can they destroy. Wind, rain, snow, and water all contribute to the slow erosion, or wearing away, of a mountain. In some cases, erosion creates valleys and canyons. Usually, it's the flow of a river that cuts valleys through mountains. Sometimes, slow-moving glaciers do the job.

The beauty and variety of landforms on Earth are truly awe-inspiring. But it doesn't stop here. Many planets have revealed spectacular "landforms" of their own.

Ll

Scientists believe that around 4.5 billion years ago, while the earth was still forming, a rock the size of Mars smashed into it. Bits of the rock and the earth catapulted into space. Eventually, these bits gathered together with the help of gravity and formed the moon. Only time will tell if this theory will prove true.

The moon's surface is much like the earth's, but there are differences. The moon's temperature ranges from a boiling 260 degrees Fahrenheit (127 degrees Celsius) to a freezing -280 degrees Fahrenheit (-173 degrees Celsius)—all in one day! And although scientists have discovered ice at the moon's poles, no other water or evidence of water has been found. The moon has no weather—no wind or heat or rain. And instead of rich, moist soil, the moon's surface is covered with gray, sandy dust called regolith. It is so dry and still that the famous footprints left by astronaut Neil Armstrong, the first human to set foot on the moon, will be visible for millions of years!

M m

M is for Moon

The moon can change from full to not,
a month is all the time it's got.
Bright enough to light the sky,
then so dark—I wonder why?

On a larger scale, the moon is always in motion. And even though the earth feels still to us, a head-spinning amount of movement is going on here as well. The earth rotates around its axis, an imaginary line that runs through the center of the planet from the North Pole to the South Pole. It takes twenty-four hours—a full day—for the earth to complete a full rotation. The moon orbits Earth, taking 29.5 days—almost a month—to complete the circle. The earth and the moon revolve around the sun, taking 365 days—a full year—to complete the circle. How we count off our days, months, and years is no accident.

While the moon is orbiting Earth, it's also rotating on its axis. It takes the moon 29.5 days to complete a full rotation—the same number of days it takes to orbit Earth. This is the reason we see only one side of the moon. And it's always the same side. Without the sun, though, we wouldn't be able to see the moon at all. The moon looks bright to us because it's reflecting the light of the sun.

The changing positions of the moon, earth, and sun in relation to each other determine how much of the moon is visible to us. These waxing and waning phases—as the moon seems to grow from a sliver to a full moon and then back again to a sliver—repeat every month. And every month, the pattern of high tide and low tide is due to the moon. The moon's gravity pulls on the earth, making ocean water bulge into tides.

The moon is the only place in outer space that we humans have visited. While we were there, we collected samples from the moon's surface for study here on Earth. We learn more every day about the world beyond. Who knows what more the moon will teach us about the outer limits.

Nn

The northern lights are a spectacular show of dancing colors in the night sky. The lights come from electrically charged particles carried by the sun's wind. These solar winds can reach speeds of 1 million miles (1.6 million kilometers) per hour! At that speed, the wind can break through the magnetic field created by the earth's core, or center. The magnetic field forms the magnetosphere. It surrounds and protects the earth.

The solar wind's electrically charged particles collide with oxygen and nitrogen in the magnetosphere. This creates light that can be seen above Earth's northern and southern magnetic poles. The northern lights are called aurora borealis (ah-ROR-ah bor-ee-AH-less). The southern lights are called aurora australis (ah-ROR-ah aw-STRAY-les).

Auroral lights can be red, green, blue, or purple. The color depends on two conditions. One is the altitude, or how high above the earth the collisions occur. And the other is whether nitrogen or oxygen is involved. These conditions form various combinations that are constantly changing. And it is these changes that produce the graceful movements of the light associated with aurora borealis.

You are more likely to see the northern lights the closer you are to the North Pole. But every once in a while, even people living in the southern states get to see a faint show of dancing light.

N is for Northern Lights

An eerie glow goes streaming by.
Colors dance high in the sky.
A nighttime show put on display
by dazzling lights that swell and sway.

Oil, natural gas, and coal are called fossil fuels. When we use fossil fuels we are actually using the energy of plants and animals from the distant past.

Millions of years ago, even before the time of dinosaurs, tiny plants and animals lived in the oceans. Many of them stored energy from the sun and carbon from the atmosphere in their bodies. Carbon is part of all life on Earth.

When these ancient organisms died, they sank to the bottom of the sea. Year after year, heavy layers of mud and rock buried them deeper into the earth. The pressure and temperature increased. After millions of years of pressure and heat, the carbon changed into oil and gas.

Deep underground, the oil oozed its way into and through the little holes of porous rock. Some oil tried to move upward but was blocked by solid rock, creating an oil reservoir. And this is the oil we drill for to use in our everyday lives.

Some oil, though, made it to the earth's surface. And in a few places, this oil formed pools we call tar pits. The oil in

O is for Oil

Oil is made on Earth, you see,
of tiny fossils from the sea.
For years and years they're pressed and heated,
they then become the oil we needed.

these pools isn't really tar, though. It's asphalt. Ancient animals would wander through a tar pit, get mired in the goopy asphalt, and die. Fossils of these animals, including mammoths and saber-toothed tigers, have been found in some tar pits. They add important information to the fossil record.

We use oil in many ways—to gas up our cars and heat our homes, of course. But oil is also used to make plastic bottles and toys. It's used in medicine and in building materials. And we have found many more uses for oil.

Oil is a nonrenewable resource. This means that the earth has only a certain amount of oil. If we use it all up, it's gone for good. It's important we use this natural resource carefully.

P is for Plate Tectonics

All together, then apart,
the earth's land changes shape.
Drifting slow in fits and starts,
the plates remake landscape.

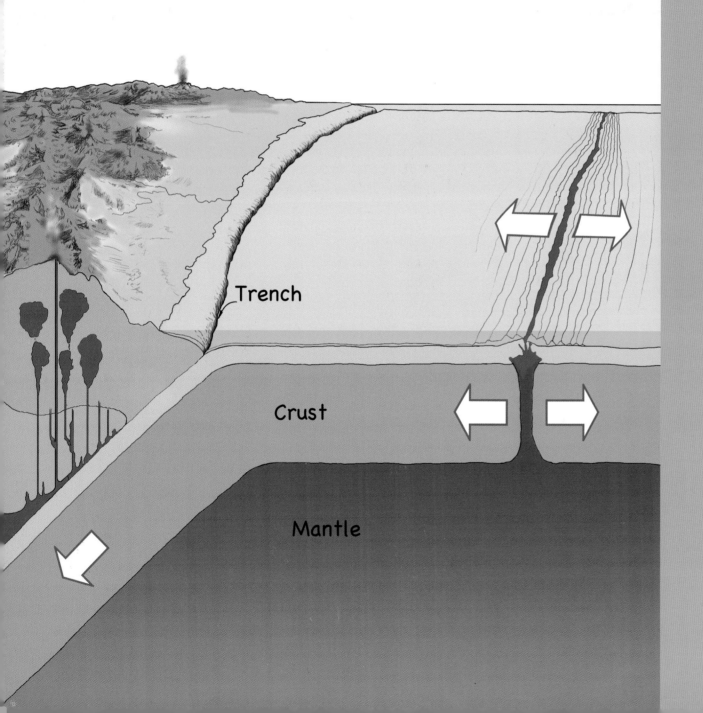

Trench

Crust

Mantle

Plate tectonics is a theory. But most scientists believe that it explains a lot about how the earth works. The theory is that the earth's crust, or outer layer, is made of rocky plates. It's as though the surface of the earth cracked into many pieces.

More than 200 million years ago, all the continents were just one big land mass called Pangaea (pan-JEE-ah). Then they started to split and drift apart, "riding" the separated plates. Eventually, the continents as we know them today were formed. Look at a map and you'll see that the continents look like puzzle pieces that could fit together.

The plates are still moving—they bang into, pull away from, or slip by each other all the time. Usually, these movements are too slow for us to notice. Sometimes, though, all this activity brings on an earthquake or causes a volcano to erupt. And over millions of years, mountains can form.

The San Andreas Fault in California is on the boundary between two plates. One plate is moving ever so slowly to the northwest. The other plate is moving slowly southward. Today, Los Angeles is about 385 miles (619 kilometers) south of San Francisco. Scientists predict that in 10 million years or so, Los Angeles and San Francisco will be right next to each other. A few million years later and Los Angeles will be north of San Francisco. What a ride!

Pp

Beware of Quicksand! warns the sign. But is quicksand all that dangerous? What is quicksand, anyway?

It's really no mystery. Quicksand is a combination of sand, clay, and salt water. It looks solid, but when you step on it, you start to sink. The sand liquefies, or becomes watery, when it's stirred up. The sand and clay sink to the bottom, and that's the muck that can trap you. But this muck keeps you from going under completely. A quicksand pit is usually pretty shallow, anyway. It would be hard to drown in one unless you fell in head-first. Besides, the human body has a lower density, or is less compact, than quicksand. You're more likely to float than to sink all the way under.

If you ever find yourself trapped in quicksand, move as little as possible. And don't let anyone try to pull you out. It's as hard to pull someone out of quicksand as it is to lift a car. The opposing forces would split you in half. All you have to do to escape quicksand is slowly move your legs around. This will bring water to the bottom and loosen the sand's grip around your legs. Then lie back and float, slowly making your way to solid land.

Q q

Q is for Quicksand

Do you sink or do you not,
quicksand holds you in one spot.
Trapped it seems, nowhere to go,
but free you'll be if you move slow.

R r

Trees so thick it's hard to see.
Wet and muggy as can be,
 plants and animals galore,
found in rainforests tree to floor.

Rainforests are home to an enormous variety of plant and animal species. So many, in fact, that we haven't discovered all of them yet. We may never discover some of them.

We're most familiar with tropical rainforests, like the Amazon. These forests grow near the equator, where it's always warm. They get an average of 80 inches (203 centimeters) of rain a year. That's a lot of rain! Hundreds of species, or kinds, of broadleaf trees grow in this balmy climate.

Life in rainforests isn't just on the ground. Four levels, from ground to treetop, provide unique living areas. Plants and animals on each level are specially suited to living there.

Many birds and insects hang out at the top of the tallest trees on the emergent level. These trees grow well above the canopy, the next level down. Most of the rainforest's treetops reach the canopy. And the canopy is home to up to 90 percent of the rainforest critters, including reptiles and mammals. Below the canopy is the cool, dark understory, where reptiles, mammals, and a large variety of insects live. The bottom level is the forest floor. It's too dark for most plants to grow here, but there are plenty of insects.

Decay is rapid on the forest floor. Once plants or animals die, they start rotting. Their nutrients are taken up quickly by the living plants to help them grow. More dead

plants means more food, hiding places, and homes for animals. Many species of the rainforest have symbiotic relationships. That means that two species work together to help each other. Some scientists say that life in the rainforest is more interconnected than in any other biome. A biome is an area with similar plants, animals, soils, and climate.

We hear a lot about rainforests because they are endangered. People are cutting down rainforest trees at an alarming rate. This removes homes for many of the unique plants and animals that live there.

We get a lot from rainforests. For instance, some of our medicines come from rainforest plants. And the forest's trees take carbon dioxide out of the air and release oxygen into the air. This helps keep air breathable all around the world. What will happen to our world if we continue to destroy the rainforest?

The sun provides energy and warmth to all life on Earth. Plants get their food energy from sunlight through photosynthesis (foh-toh-SIN-theh-sis). This energy is passed on to animals when they eat plants. And the ways the sun and the earth relate to each other affect our weather, climate, seasons, and daily patterns of light and dark.

The sun is the center of our solar system and the closest star to Earth. Its gravity keeps our solar system together. Although it's a medium-sized star, the sun is huge compared to the earth. One million Earths could fit into a hollowed-out sun!

The sun isn't hollow, though. It's a ball of fiery-hot hydrogen and helium gas. In the core, or center, of the sun, nuclear reactions are turning the hydrogen into helium. And that's what creates the sun's glowing heat.

The sun is changing all the time. Storms create dark, cooler areas called sunspots, and once in a while solar flares burst from the sun. These activities cause auroras (ah-ROR-ahz) and can knock out our electricity.

Every once in a while we experience a solar eclipse. The moon lines up between the earth and the sun. When the moon blocks the sun entirely, complete darkness can descend upon the earth.

Don't ever look directly at the sun, though, not even during an eclipse. Although the sun is nearly 93 million miles (about 150 million kilometers) from the earth, it's bright enough to damage your eyes.

Ss

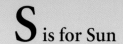

S is for Sun

Star, star, burning bright,
the sun is full of heat and light.
Without the sun I'd greatly fear,
life on Earth would not be here.

T is for Tides

Surging high and ebbing low,
the moon creates the tides, you know.
Its gravity's the reason why
tides can be so very high.

There's a beautiful "dance" that the moon, sun, and earth perform. The moon and the earth spin and twirl around the sun and around each other, creating a continuous display of light and dark, high tide and low tide. And in the midst of it all is gravity.

Gravity is the force that holds us on Earth and keeps the planets together in our solar system. And it's the force that creates the tides. Don't confuse tides with waves. Waves are caused by wind, storms, and currents. They occur all the time. Tides are formed when the moon's gravity pulls at Earth, making water bulge. This happens on the opposite side of the earth as well. The earth is always rotating in its dance with the sun and moon, creating two high tides and two low tides each day.

High tides bring fresh seawater to tide pools that form along rocky shores. Small marine plants and animals such as sea cucumbers and starfish live in these small pools nestled among rocks. Female sea turtles depend on high tides to carry them to shore so they can lay their eggs.

Tides are important in the lives of many marine animals. Tides even provide recreation for people. How amazing that the moon, with a little help from the sun, makes it all happen. Surf's up!

Most of us walk around not thinking about what's under our feet. We don't wonder what's under the grass and soil that makes up the earth's surface. But there are 4,000 miles (6,435 kilometers) between where we're standing and the earth's core. There's got to be something really cool lurking in all that space.

Actually, there's something really hot. The earth is made of three basic layers—the crust, the mantle, and the core. The crust is the outer layer, the part that we live on. It's very thin compared to the other layers. The mantle is right underneath, and it accounts for 83 percent of the earth's mass. It's divided into two parts. The upper mantle is brittle, and makes up the tectonic plates that keep Earth on the move. It floats on the lower mantle. This layer is made of molten rock called magma, which has a peanut butter–like consistency. Deeper still is the outer core, made of iron and a bit of nickel. It's so hot that the iron and nickel have melted. It is responsible for Earth's magnetic fields. And at the very center is the inner core made of even hotter iron and nickel. It's under a lot of pressure, though, so it remains solid.

So now we know what's underfoot. Thankfully, the earth's surface has cooled enough that our feet don't get burned!

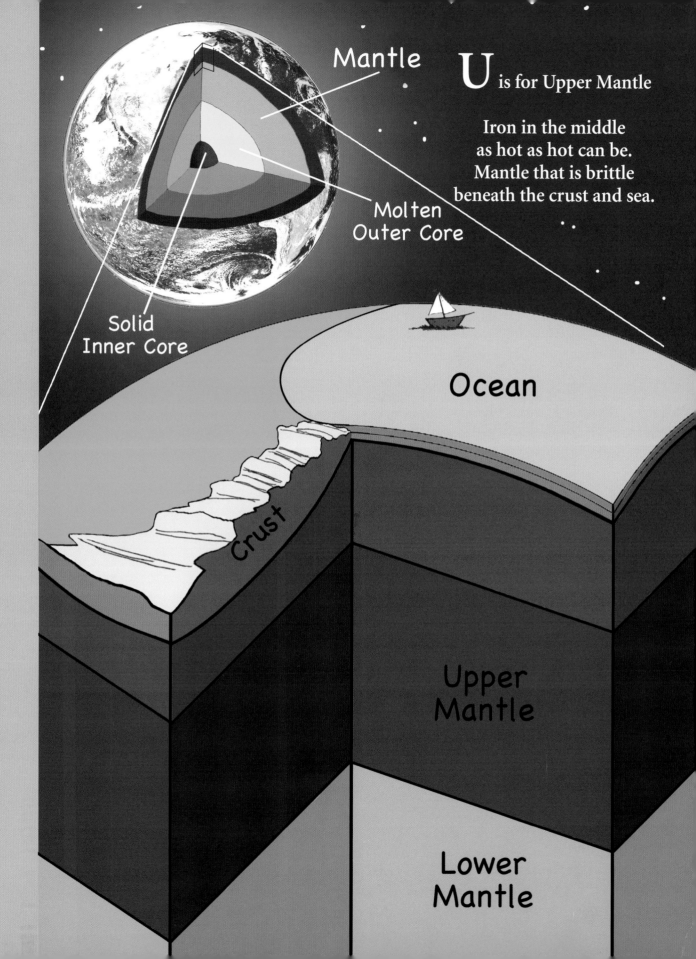

Mantle

U is for Upper Mantle

Iron in the middle
as hot as hot can be.
Mantle that is brittle
beneath the crust and sea.

Molten
Outer Core

Solid
Inner Core

Ocean

Crust

Upper
Mantle

Lower
Mantle

U u

An erupting volcano is a dramatic show of Earth's power. But not all volcanoes are massive explosions of ash and rock. Not all spew out hot flowing lava that ravages everything in its path. Some ooze lava without producing much of a ruckus at all. But whether they erupt or ooze, all volcanoes begin with heated, softened rock called magma deep inside the Earth.

The earth's core, or center, heats the layer of rocky mantle right next to it. The rock melts and becomes magma. Gases are released during this process. Pressure builds from the heat and gases. Magma is pushed upward and forced through vents or cracks in the earth's crust, or surface. Once magma comes out of the earth, it's called lava. It then hardens on the cool surface of the earth or underwater on the ocean floor.

Volcanoes both destroy and build. Lava, especially the fast-moving sort, can destroy everything in its path. Whole cities, civilizations even, have been wiped out by this liquid fire and its hot gases. Wind can carry volcanic ash all around the world and can affect an area's climate for a few years. If deep enough, ash can smother plants and animals. But it also builds up and fertilizes the land, creating nutrient-rich soil for growing crops. Without question, volcanoes are awesome works of nature.

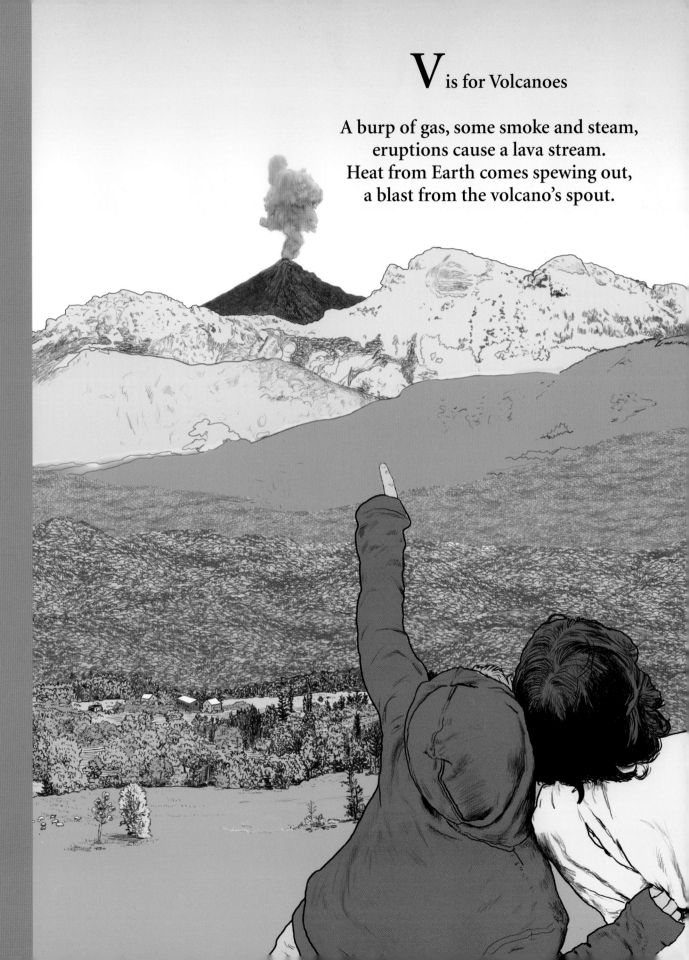

V is for Volcanoes

A burp of gas, some smoke and steam,
eruptions cause a lava stream.
Heat from Earth comes spewing out,
a blast from the volcano's spout.

Water is a basic ingredient for life. And it's the only substance we know of that can exist naturally as a gas, a liquid, and a solid. So it's not surprising that water is all around us. It's in the air and under the ground. It flows down rivers and is stored in oceans. It's trapped in glaciers and even inside our bodies. Most amazing of all—the water you drink today is the same water that was slurped up by dinosaurs millions of years ago!

The continuous change of water from liquid to gas to solid is called the water cycle, or the hydrologic cycle. Energy from the sun powers the cycle. The sun warms the earth, changing some liquid water to water vapor, or gas, in a process called evaporation. The water evaporates into the air, where winds can carry it anywhere in the world.

Water vapor in the air cools as it rises and condenses into tiny water droplets that form clouds. When a cloud gets too heavy with water, it rains, snows, hails, or otherwise drops the water back down to Earth. This is called precipitation.

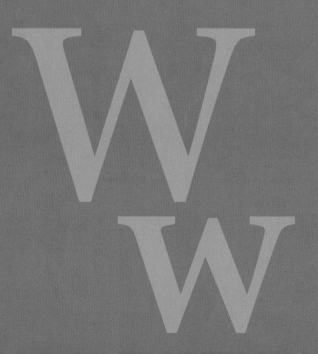

W is for Water Cycle

Liquid, gas, and solid—water is all three.
In the air and on the ground,
in a cycle round and round,
collected in the sea.

Some precipitation falls into oceans, lakes, or other bodies of water. Some falls on land. Water can freeze into a glacier and be trapped there for thousands of years as a solid. It can seep into the ground and become groundwater. Groundwater makes it back up to the earth's surface through plants, springs, and even volcanoes. Water can flow downhill as runoff and end up in rivers, which eventually carry water to oceans. Water can be stored in oceans for thousands of years. At any one time, Earth's water is going through every stage of the water cycle.

We must be careful, though. Water is a non-renewable resource. That means the water now on Earth is all there ever was, and it is all there ever will be. This is why it's so important for us to keep our water clean and not be wasteful. If we don't use water wisely, we may someday run out of fresh, clean water.

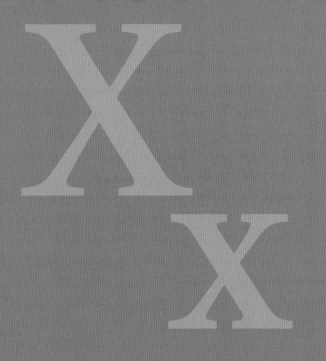

Have you ever wondered how spindly plants can stand upright, or how water gets to the tippy-top of giant-sized trees? It all has to do with xylem (ZI-lem).

Most plants are vascular plants. They have tubes called vessels that direct water and nutrients to all their parts. Xylem is one type of vessel. As water evaporates from leaves, more water is drawn upward from the roots through the xylem. Xylem also helps keep the plant's stem rigid and standing upright.

The other type of vessel is phloem (FLOH-em). Leaves soak up sunlight and change its energy to food. This process is called photosynthesis (foh-toh-SIN-theh-sis). Phloem tubes distribute these nutrients to the rest of the plant. A tree's sap comes through its phloem.

In trees, the inner bark is made of phloem. The wood is made of xylem. In places with distinct seasons, a tree grows during the summer and is dormant, or not growing, during the winter. This cycle forms rings in the wood, which are visible on a cut tree trunk. Each ring represents one year of the tree's life. So the next time you see a fallen tree, you can count its rings and find out how old it was—all because of xylem!

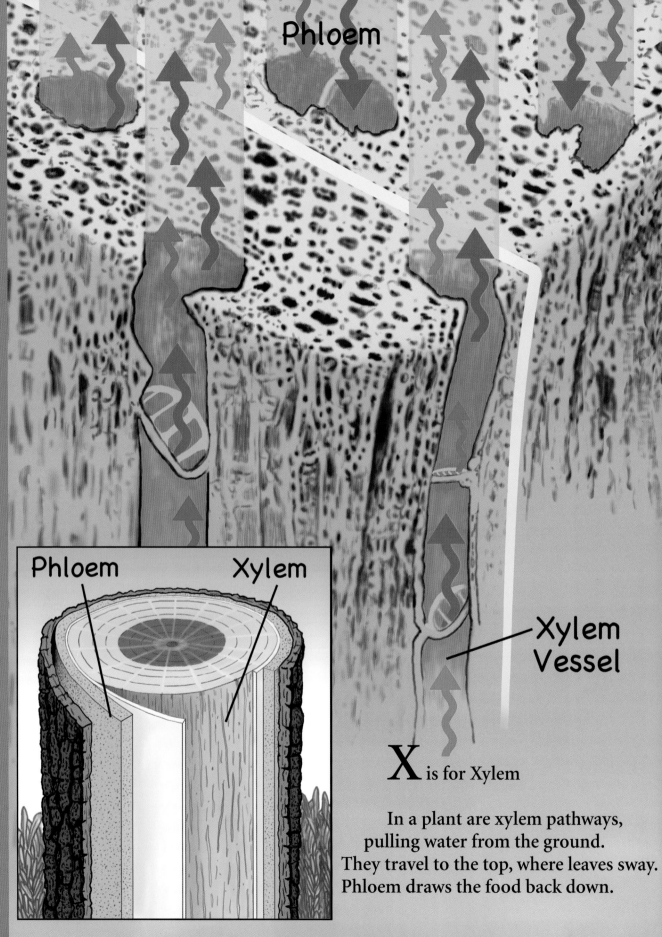

Phloem

Phloem   Xylem

Xylem Vessel

X is for Xylem

In a plant are xylem pathways,
pulling water from the ground.
They travel to the top, where leaves sway.
Phloem draws the food back down.

Geysers are rare. Those that erupt on a fairly regular basis are rarer still. The most famous geyser is Old Faithful in Yellowstone National Park. This geyser "faithfully" erupts every 30 to 120 minutes, or so.

About half of the world's 1,000 geysers can be found at Yellowstone National Park in Wyoming. Geysers tend to form at the edges of tectonic plates or above hot spots. These are areas heated by magma that are just below the earth's surface. Much of Yellowstone sits atop such hot spots.

Underground water deep inside the earth becomes hot as it flows near magma. The superheated water rises through cracks and passageways that lead upward. Some passageways become narrow. Pressure builds and forces the hot, bubbling, steamy water through the narrow passageway. This causes steam and water to erupt from the geyser with jaw-dropping power. As a matter of fact, a geyser's energy can be collected and is called geothermal energy.

Geysers can be quite dramatic. In Old Faithful's case, up to 8,000 gallons (30,285 liters) of water shoot 100 to 180 feet (30 to 55 meters) up into the air. Adding to the drama is the fact that this water is about 500 years old! It takes that long for water to soak into the ground, become heated, and find its way back to the earth's surface.

Y is for Yellowstone's Old Faithful

Water, heat, and pressure's brewing.
Steam is building up 'til—wow!
Underground it all was stewing,
then erupting water—POW!

Z is for Zones

Rain or snow or warm may be
daily weather we can see.
Record the weather year to year—
climates and their zones appear.

Everyone knows what weather is. Just a peek outside gives us clues. Is the sun shining? Is it raining? Temperature and humidity are just two of the conditions that form our day-to-day weather.

But what's the difference between weather and climate? Basically, climate is the trend of weather patterns in any particular area. So if you live where there are long, snowy winters, you live in a cold climate.

Scientists have different ways to classify the world's climates. Some scientists separate climates into five zones: tropical, dry, mild, snowy, and polar. All the places around the world that share the same weather patterns also share the same climate zone.

The angle at which the sun's rays hit different parts of the earth influences the climate. The most direct rays hit the tropical equator. The equator is the midpoint of the earth between the South and North Poles. The sun's rays hit the South and North Poles at a lesser angle, contributing to their cold polar climate.

Being aware of our climate helps us choose what to hang in our closets. We don't need heavy winter coats if we live in the southern United States, for instance. Climate also affects the kinds of plants and animals that live in any given region. You're not going to find a kangaroo living wild in Alaska. Knowing about climate zones helps us understand our world a little better.

1) Tropical
- frequent rain
- temperatures over 64.4°F

2) Dry
- moisture evaporates more than it rains
- much of Africa and the Middle East are dry

3) Mild
- much of the U.S. and Europe are mild
- largest climate sections

4) Snowy
- high temperatures rarely go above 50°F

5) Polar
- coldest areas
- much of Canada, Alaska, the Arctic, and Antarctica
- never above 50°F

What Does Climate Change Mean?

Climate change has been a naturally occurring event throughout the earth's history. Eras of ice ages have melted into periods of warmth and then cooled again into other ice ages. Environmentalists and many scientists have alerted us to what they see as an unnatural rise in temperature. They've pointed out that the earth has warmed by 1.0 to 1.7 degrees Fahrenheit (-17.2 to -16.8 degrees Celsius) over the past 100 years. This is the same time period that factories, cars, and other fossil fuel burners were invented. Fossil fuels produce greenhouse gases such as carbon dioxide and methane. These gases get trapped in Earth's atmosphere and warm it up. Normally, the earth depends on greenhouse gases to keep it warm enough to support life. But the additional gases spewed by our modern machinery are speeding up the warming trend, some scientists believe. Other scientists insist that the warming trend we're seeing is quite natural. They believe science and history prove we're merely experiencing a warm period between ice ages. Without knowing for sure the exact reasons for climate change, we do need to consider the impact our human activity has on the rest of Earth.

Other Earth Science Facts:

Amber stores static electricity and when rubbed it attracts lint.

The youngest fossils are 10,000 years old; the oldest are more than 3 billion years old. The oldest fossils are buried deepest in the ground, and it's the earth surrounding a fossil that gives scientists clues to its age.

When you're in a desert and you see a pool of water off in the distance, what are you really seeing? You're in the desert, after all, where water is hard to find. This neat trick of nature is the result of sunlight reflecting off the hot air that is rising above the ground. Such visions are called mirages.

The massive 8.8 earthquake that hit Chile on February 27, 2010, was strong enough to change the rate of the earth's rotation and shorten the length of each day by 1.26 microsecond!